Landscaping Ideas

THE BEST LANDSCAPING GUIDE
TO QUICKLY ENHANCE YOUR
YARD. DISCOVER BEAUTIFUL
AND SMART WAYS TO CREATE
PERFECT GARDENS FOR YOUR
BACKYARD & FRONTYARD

Landscape Design Academy

Table of Contents

INTRODUCTION

When I speak of landscapes, I think of something between these two extremes. You must dream a little when designing your home garden, but of course, your plans must be rooted in reality. The landscape is the general outdoor environment. It can also refer to large parks and open spaces or smaller urban areas. We usually do not have much control over the broader landscape design. However, we have full control over the "patio" or the immediate environment around our home. Why not make the most of it? Make it more attractive, more pleasant. Make it special!

I prefer the term "home garden" to the term "patio" or "landscape". My idea for a garden is not just a vegetable bed.

When I talk about the home garden, I represent images of sidewalks, living areas, open view or personal data protection screens, attractive little spaces with impressive features such as a statuette, plant, or innovative fountain. That's all about it. It is the view from the street or the view from the kitchen window. With that in mind, landscaping is much more than just decoration. We can do whatever we want. Your outdoor living space should be a continuation of the home interior and not only match but also add style to the house.

The typical American landscape style emphasizes the appearance of the house from the street. The "public space", the street perspective, is generally designed to decorate the home creating a "call for restraint". However, there would be a wall near the road in many other countries in the world with plantings within the wall that creates a view of the garden from inside the house.

When you think about it, your home is your castle. It is your most significant advantage. It is your refuge from the "jungle". There you relax, rejuvenate and entertain your friends. You live here! Just Do your best to make your home cozy for visitors. Make it comfortable, enjoyable, and exciting. Make it exciting!

Okay, now that we're starting to see the big picture, what about this "rooted in reality" idea? A well-

designed landscape should do more than decorate your home. Well covered, it will withstand a host of adverse conditions. Well-designed beds will make cutting and maintenance much simpler. Runners should facilitate movement around their home and welcome visitors. Are you starting to get an idea? Many features of the landscape can be an asset or a liability. It is all a matter of where to plant and where. I think you would agree that it is quite important to deserve a well thought out plan.

As mentioned above, a well-designed garden area should provide beauty, privacy, relaxation, fun, and fun for many more years. It is not a short-term proposal. The development of the garden takes years. We deal with trees here. Unfortunately, in our American mobile society, many people think short term. We often intend to move in a few years for various reasons. But even in this case, the right landscape will offer a few years of enjoyment and return on investment when you sell. But the great rewards come after many years of cultivation and development of a properly designed, installed and maintained garden. This can really lead to an increase in your enjoyment and quality of life more than just increasing the value of your property!

Always take into considerations the needs of everyone who will be enjoying the elegant garden escape. You need to take into consideration the

safety of your design if you have children,. Then a water feature without a basin may be better suited than a pond for families with small children or if you have a dog pet that likes to play in your flowerbeds then it may be best to reconsider delicate flowers that will only be trampled.

Lastly, you must also consider any storage you may need. If you have furniture for garden that is not weatherproof, you may need to make room for a shed that can store the furniture, bikes, toys for your pool, etc...

The design of your elegant garden should be made to fit your space, large or small. If, for instance, you have a view then you will want to craft a relaxing space that opens up toward the view. If you instead are surrounded by nosy neighbors, you may want to create a sense of privacy around a central area. Creating the perfect elegant garden is a combination of plants and ambience. Ambience is the result of the whole project. This means the manner in which the plants flows together, the shape of the garden, the lighting, any water features, furniture, and accessories. You can mix and match colors and styles to create unique ambiences all their own. You can mix and match materials such as concrete, rocks, stone, or wood.

There are numerous materials you can use in your elegant landscaping garden. Composite bender

boards are the best for footpaths and walkways as well because it doesn't rot and it bends easily. Wood would rot and does not bend as much. It must be replaced often. Concrete can be decorative but it isn't exquisite. Stones and pavers are also lovely.

Now, if you feel like it, you can make sure that every bit of the garden shows some exciting feature or plant in the various seasons. This kind of seasonal garden look is one of landscaping ideas that you can try. Various landscaping ideas that you can try are on this books. However, many of these ideas may require you to spend loads of money, but you can try others too. These landscaping ideas, whether they are simple or complex, have the same end goal in sight, making your garden look unique.

CHAPTER 1
How to Design Your Landscape

What Is Landscaping?

Landscaping is normally defined as any activity which alters the visible characteristics of a piece of land. It can be anything, then, really. Anything which changes the appearance of a piece of land is considered a form of landscaping. It can be planting a tree, putting bushes, adding rocks or pieces of wood or it can be as easy as changing the slope of the field from flat to hilly or from hill to flat.

You can play around with living elements such as flowers or trees in landscaping or use natural elements such as rocks for your desired effect. Anyone can do the landscaping; all they need is a clear view of what you want it to look like once it's finished, a bit of art and a bit of a green thumb of course.

In any project, the first step is knowing your area. Depending on where you live the art of creating something beautiful will change. Things that grow wondrously in California may never get to bud if, for example, you plant them in Michigan. Take into account, therefore, the weather patterns and the various features such as soil quality, frost line depth, winds, and native flora that will do well within your area. Above all, pack your patience!

When your plan is in place, you can set to work. Sometimes you need to reshape the land you want to landscape, and this is called grading. Sometimes you'll need to fill up areas with extra topsoil or take out rocks and weeds before you start, but most of all, it's a chance to be creative and have fun in a natural setting.

Landscaping takes time, and at least you need to have a little sense of what you're doing. But don't worry if you can't get it right, we've got qualified landscapers for this. They will come in and evaluate your space and give you plenty of choices about what to do to make it as beautiful as it can be. They've seen it all before and are going to be there for repairs if you need it over the changing seasons too.

The development of an area is not simple and requires a great deal of consideration. But there are people with the ability who are inborn. And there

are those who gain expertise in this area too. If you aren't one of these people and need to develop your yard, you can employ the assistance of experts who offer these kinds of services.

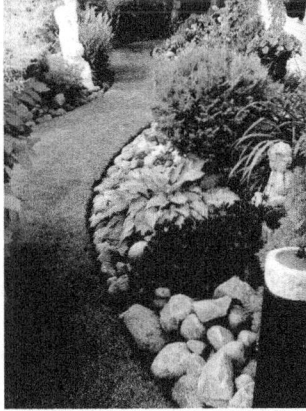

The Most Important Design Principles

Shape

Most of the landscape artists referred this as the most important design principle to get right. By means of the empty areas of space within a garden like your patio and lawn areas. Mainly, its the shapes you create inside of the garden counts, so it's really doesn't matter what actual shape your garden is. Before you start with the design, you have to create the right shape. It will serve as the foundation whereas other design principles may interact with it. So, again, you really need to have the right shape in place before you use the other design principles.

Proportion

With this, you need to make sure the empty areas are in the right proportion to the planted areas once you have the right shape for the areas of empty space within your garden, the lawn and patios. You have to keenly whether the planting borders are too big or too small. If failed to do so, even if you have come up with the perfect design shape, the garden won't look and feel right.

Proportion comes into play with upright structures like arches, walls, and pergolas. So it's very important that these are in the right proportion to the surroundings and the users.

Movement

It may seem like an odd thing to think about in what is essentially a stationary object. The type of movement that is referring to is on how the garden flows from one point to another visually. If you see an entire garden in one go, it will looks like a dull garden but if certain design tricks are used, you can guide the eye where you want it to go with the shapes you've used and this will create more interest.

By skillfully using repeat planting, it can also create a sense of movement. Once seen, it will automatically jump from one group to the next of the same plant up the garden.

Punctuation

This could be included in movement. Mostly, people punctuate their garden with focal points like statues and urns in all the wrong places, missing wonderful opportunities to create exciting points of interest of garden.

One of the finishing touches to a good design is when the statue or feature plant are carefully placed. Thereafter, the correct piece that is in right position can beautifully transform a garden. When used correctly, focal points can be very dramatic at changes in direction or end of views. It will also lead the eye around the garden to create a sense of movement.

Balance

You'll hear it often on designers talk about balance. This is one of the more subtle elements to have good designs and several things can affect balance. There's visual balance, which is created by getting the correct proportion, but there is also a 'shape balance' to consider. Not having many elements within the design affects the balance. Making the design that is not top heavy with the shape is important.

Repetition

Plants can help create balance and harmony in a design when used it correctly. For example, repeating certain design elements, shapes, textures. It also helps with clarity and movement. So, you need to be very careful not to overdo it. It will bring us nicely onto our final main principle.

Simplicity

So one of the main keys to good design is keeping things simple really is. Everything you put on will have a much better chance of working if the underlying design shape is simple. If it happens that the main shapes of your design are fussy and too busy, the whole design will look and feel chaotic.

Understanding My Garden Soil

To have a good garden, soil that is healthy, well-drained and with a high content of organic material must be given. The garden's success is all in field planning.

Checking soil pH

It is critical that soil has the correct pH balance. Getting the soil analyzed every three years is recommended. There are pH kits available that let you to check the soil yourself or the local agricultural school or soil survey office can do the soil analysis for you. A report will be returned to the applicant for soil and will contain guidelines for elevating or lowering the soil pH if the pH is not within the acceptable amount.

The soil's Ph. may be increased by adding lime to the soil, and the pH may be lowered by adding Sulphur or peat moss to the soil. For some planting types, the report may mention the optimum pH of the soil. When that does not happen, the pH value can be quickly looked up. While applying lime to the soil, a general rule of thumb is to use 4 pounds of product per 100 square feet of soil for each point where the pH is below 6.5 and use 1 pound of Sulphur per 100 square feet of soil for each point above 7.5.

Preparing the Ground

Replace the grass cover from the garden area with a grub how and use the clods to patch or throw other pieces of the lawn into the compost pile, if you have one. Upon cutting the grass loosen the soil to approximately 15 inches deep. Soil loosening may be achieved with hand tools such as a spade or pitchfork, depending on the size of the garden. If you have a big garden, you can consider renting a motorized rototiller to do the job.

Add in compost content after the soil has been loosened, to add nutrients to the soil. When there are to be at least a few days or more before the garden is planted, cover the garden soil with a mulch layer, around 2 to 3 inches thick. The mulch prevents the weeds from being created and prevents the soil moist. The mulch would also

protect the soil from disease and keep soil temperature relatively stable.

Mulch Versions

The type of mulch to use can be wood chips, wood bark shredded, pine needles, straw, or hay. Mulching leaves with a mulching mower or mulching vac are likewise ideal types of mulch. All of these items can be purchased in the local home improvement store's lawn and garden department, a plant and landscaping shop and even from your own backyard. Growing planting season should be replaced with mulch. In the spring, it can be raked out until the soil is prepared for the planting season to come. If the mulch is a compostable material like shredded leaves, straw or hay, in fall, it can be turned back into the soil.

Fertilizers

Fertilizer contributes nutrients to the soil. Compost is a healthy fertilizer and should be applied to the soil every year as the soil prepares for the new season of planting. Other types of fertilizer may also need to be added, depending on the soil type. Blood meal and bone meal are great organic fertilizers and do not add toxic substances to the soil. The application of fertilizer is achieved during the growing season by hoeing a trench about 3 to 4 inches deep adjacent to the row of plants, without damaging the plants. In the trench, apply the

fertilizer, and cover with dirt. Rain or irrigation can allow the fertilizer to work into the soil.

You may think that your region has the most daunting soil problems but be assured that you are not alone. In hopes of providing a detailed understanding of the process, we will debate in detail the how's and whys of soil preparation. The steps to take when preparing the soil for planting:

Clean off current vegetation.

When the soil exceeds 8-12 "depth.

Remove one or two inches of organic material.

Add 1-2 "of loam of sand.

Add 20-30 pounds per 1000 square feet of gypsum.

Garnish with fertilizer.

Till the soil between steps.

Remove the existing vegetation with a hoe or bladed shovel. Be especially aware of Bermuda grass being sure to remove all the grass runners. Some home gardeners prefer using a non-selective herbicide to perform this process. Pay particular attention to the term "non-selective" and take it at face value. The herbicide will kill anything green.

The method used for soil preparation is very basic, 1/3 organic material, 1/3 sandy loam, and 1/3 clay soil. Organic material refers to a once-living product of nature. The strongest and most widely used is peat

moss that can be bought at the local home supply store. Peat moss is made of partly decayed wood and plant material.

Sandy loam can be bought and shipped from a local manufacturer of topsoil and sands. It varies from true sand because its composition is made up of equal parts of sand, silt, and clay. Purchasing "play sand" bags do not yield the same results.

Gypsum is classified as an additive to help loosen the soil. In the spirit of honesty and total transparency, its use is not widely accepted. The substance has been used effectively, achieving outstanding results. This does not include substantial nutrients but, if used, will provide a tremendous improvement in the looseness and quality of the soil.

Few clay soils are rich enough to stand alone and adequately sustain plant life, so the plants rely on us, the home gardener, to provide what the soil can't do. We, in effect, look to fertilizers. Fertilizing a lawn, garden or flower bed always seems to raise the question of what kind of nutrients are required and how do I know?

Many people are concerned about the rise in soil volume created by applying organic material and sandy loam to the current soil. It should be remembered that this method means that you are not planning acres and acres of soil but a few

hundred square feet of greenhouse, landscaping, or flower beds. Don't worry. The process mentioned would cause an increase in the ground level of inches and not feet.

These folks have followed strict realistic and educational criteria and can have the best base of expertise for you. Through troublesome foundation detection and problem-solving, you can be amazed at their capabilities.

Anything you may think maybe a challenge may also be an advantage. Hard black clay soil can present challenges, but your garden or flower beds will be safe, efficient and add beauty and fun for your lawn and life with a little experience and hard work.

Climate for landscaping

Wind

One of the major hazards of the new garden is wind, particularly in a newly developed area where natural vegetation has been removed, and the only protection round the garden is a chain link fence. The answer to this problem is to plant a dense windbreak of trees or shrubs to shelter the garden and those who use it. Evergreen shrubs provide excellent shelter.

Frost

Plants seem to be very variable in their resistance to frost some varieties thriving for a considerable number of winters only to die suddenly and leave a hole in a rapidly developing group. It is better to plant a hardy shrub than a soft thing, which has to be covered with a plastic bag all winter.

Shade

Neighboring trees or buildings may cause shade. The amount of sunlight excluded from the garden will vary not only to the size of the neighbor, but also less obviously, according to the time of the year. Plants that will grow, therefore, will depend on the other factors besides their ability to withstand shade.

Atmosphere

In some urban areas smoke pollution or the heavy chemical content of the atmosphere are injurious to many plants. Generally evergreen and conifers suffer most under these conditions since the atmosphere deposits prevent them from breathing through their leaves. Deciduous trees that lose their leaves regularly are therefore more reliable in such cases.

Noise

This is a fairly new hazard of modern living, which one needs increasingly to hold at bay. A thick planting of evergreen shrubs and trees combined with ground shaping provides an excellent baffle and cuts down noise considerably.

Seasons

The seasons as a whole divided into six seasons, each season consisting of two months and having

its own importance in landscape. The different colours of flowering, trees in the different seasons give its own impression to the environment & also in the human life.

Soil

The type of soil also affects the growth of the plant. Some plants can grow easily in sandy soils while others cannot. Similarly some plants can grow in acidic soil or clayey soil while others cannot.

Water requirement

Certain plants require more water and thus should not be planted in a hot dry climate where water is already scarce.

Size, color, form and texture of the plant

The above stated criteria in connection with the plant is to be considered and the suitability of the plant for the desired function shall be seen.

The Materials/Tools

Tools for working the soil

The main tools are used to work the soil, to plant and maintain plants.

Gardening begins with working the soil. For this, five tools are essential: a spade, a fork-spade, a hoe, a claw and a rake.

- Spade: Flat and equipped with a long handle, it is mainly used to dig the earth, while the spade fork will be used instead to spade. In most cases, the spade can replace the shovel.

- Spade fork: fitted with four flat tines and a long handle, it is the best tool for spading, less tiring than a spade.

- Hoe: equipped with a flat edge and a long handle, it allows both hoeing (breaking the crust of the soil) and weeding (eliminating weeds). At first, we can do without the weeder and use the hoe for hoeing and weeding. The hoe can be replaced by the even more versatile mop: it is a very narrow hoe, the side opposite to that of the blade is equipped with two long teeth.

- Claw: Provided with four curved teeth and a long handle, the claw is used to loosen and crumble the soil, after the passage of the spade fork and before the passage of the rake. It also makes it possible to collect the roots and to bury compost or fertilizer.

- Rake: the basic model, essential, is a rake with straight teeth, which is used to remove stones and plant debris, as well as to refine the surface layer of the soil.

Planting tools

- The dibber is a conical tool, with which a hole is made in the ground to transplant the seedlings into clods or bare roots from the seedlings.

- The transplanter is a small shovel, useful for digging the earth in order to plant or transplant.

- Not essential, the bulb planter is very practical: it allows you to make a hole equivalent to 2 or 3 times the height of the bulb and place the bulb at the bottom.

Garden maintenance tools

- A pruner allows you to cut the stems and cut the branches. It's the accessory to always have in your pocket.

- A watering can and a garden hose are essential.

- Some gloves protect effectively the tools handle the friction and are helpful to prevent blisters.

- Finally, as soon as your garden is a little larger than a pocket square , a wheelbarrow can carry all the loads.

Maintenance of gardening tools

Once a year, or more if necessary:

- Sharpen sharp tools.

- Grease the metal part of the tools.

- Grease the pruning shears.

Designing With Plants

Shape

First is the shape of the plant. Trees with a strong characteristic shape have been considered and given key positions in the skeleton planting of the garden. The weeping form is well known, but there are other forms which trees take in maturity: the umbrella shape, for example, or flat top and contrasted with these, the fastigiated (or upright) forms, ranging from the narrow column to the pyramid. Such extreme shapes are only for occasional use as a special point of emphasis.

Pattern

Akin to the overall form of a plant is its leaf form or pattern. It is quite a range of subjects from trees to herbaceous material, while not having a

particularly interesting general shape, have leaves, seed heads, or barks which are their main features.

Texture

The texture of the leaf of a plant is not only a tactile quality but also a visual one, which can add to the textural quality of the whole garden.

Color

The best and most important factor with which one works in building up a satisfactorily plant arrangement is colour -flower colour. The rules for plant selection work in the same way for any types of vegetation in any climate. In a hot climate color can be used to cool: brilliant splashes in full summer sunshine, pale color in shadow. Cacti in a desert garden should however be grouped according to their one variety contrasting with other.

Shade

There are many, including the elderly, who cannot sit in full sun, and welcome shade. It is not always an adverse characteristic in a garden and should be considered with planting design. In hotter climates shade is a basic necessity and should be provided for.

Creating a Plan

The best place to begin is to come up to an idea. So you have to think, how your front yard would really look like. Are you that this is something you want instantly? Are you really willing to work on it for a few years? or Do you want a more conservative brick walkway lined with flowers or a pre-historic jungle ones? These are the typical few questions you need to ask to yourself before you start a front or backyard landscaping project.

After having a general idea, you can now start laying out what you desire to see in your front or back yard. Everything that you want to see depending on what area you want to put it in. Shrubs are normally a common choice that looks good, and the staple of landscaping if you will. Aside from that, it will be a good idea if you try to match your landscaping that will complement the front of your house with colors, designs, and various other criteria same with the outdoor space on the back of your house.

Now, for those of us with negative fashion sense or color coordination, there is a plethora of designer help tips on the internet to help us with our front landscaping deficiency. From what plants to use, to the best arrangement, to how to place the plants that match the house – if you want it, they've got it.

The first stop is Better Homes and Gardens, or bhg.com. This is essentially the one stop shop for all

your front landscaping needs in terms of materials, but also in less tangible materials, such as general guidance do's and don'ts for landscaping and, of course, the ever present helpful tips.

If you want some great ideas of places to start, check out servicemagic.com, which has a large database of photos from other's front yard landscaping. This can be a great resource of ideas, materials, tips, and basically anything else you want for your front yard landscaping project. The great way to learn it is to observe those who are already proficient at what they do, and this is no exception. Learn from the best and adapt their ideas to your own.

How Long Does It Take To Build A Garden?

Well it really depends on how big your yard that needs to build a garden, the type of materials that will be use as well as the garden style that you want to take into effect. Usually, a minimum of 4 months starting from the first meeting and discussion up to the finished garden. In those 4 months it breaks down into 4 weeks, 2-3 weeks, 6-8 weeks and lastly, another 4 weeks. The first said weeks would be for the design process, next is for appointing of contractors then a waiting time and the last weeks is for build time. So if you want to get your design be done as early as possible, you need to brainstorm or picture what would be the style of garden you want to implement based on the design principles and communicate it to your designer and seek advice. So that the flow, the phase and the target time of building your garden will go smoothly.

CHAPTER 2
Plan Your Garden

Garden Style: How to Build It

Phasing the work

Approaches

- If it's a large garden, identify a particular area and complete it in all respects from paving through to planting. The rest of the garden could be put down to grass, used for vegetables or kept bare.

- Divide the work according to different elements or types of construction and complete several each year. For example in one year you might build the patio and path while the next year you might build an arch or a water feature.

Gardening Preparation and Timing

- Avoid using wet concrete or mortar when temperature is at or near freezing point.

- Whenever possible, try not to work during the depths of winter as it is difficult or almost impossible to work on solid frozen ground.

- Soil preparation is essential. Soil forms the backbone of the garden and gives plants the very best chance to survive in a healthy environment instead of watching them die a slow death. Proper soil preparation of the soil base in your landscape can make the difference between the success of your plants and complete failure. By analyzing the existing soil quality you may add soil conditioners. Amendment depends on soil structure, soil acidity or alkalinity and the choice of plants to be grown.

Eliminate weeds before planting.

Heavy soils benefit from being roughly dug in autumn and left to weather in winter frost and ice.

You have to plant between autumn and spring since most plants are dormant thus less weeds. However contain grown plants can be planted all year round.

Leveling Uneven ground

This mostly involves the topography of the land, for instance you for a steep slope you may add a terrace or you may add interest to your landscape by making a raised bed.

Draining the ground

- On very heavy clay soils, digging in large amounts of coarse grit helps drainage.

- For surface drainage problem, slope the soil to produce a slight fall, allowing the water to run away in drains or ditches.

- Grow crops in raised beds or ridges to keep roots drier. Water can be channeled away in the bottom of the ridge.

- Install a system of chain pipes if the water table is too close to the surface and slope.

- Slope trenches gently to the lowest point in the garden.

- If there is no natural outlet such as a ditch or a stream, construct a French drain(grave-filled)

Mulching

It is very important since it prevents loss of moisture by water evaporation from the soil surface into the atmosphere by covering it with mulch. It

also improves soil compost, for instance if leaf mold is used as the mulch. In as much as it improves surface drainage, it also suppresses weeds that compete with your garden plants for water.

Always apply mulch to damp soil; otherwise you might reduce the amount of rain reaching the soil. E.g. you can add after spring after the ground has warmed up.

There are two types of mulch, namely:

- Organic- wood chippings, farmyard manure, coarse back and leaf mold.

- Inorganic- Grit, pebbles, black plastic.

Mediterranean Garden

john scratchley photography

The extraordinary beauty of the Mediterranean-style gardens is due to the unique climate that allows the inhabitants of Spain, France, Italy and Greece to create comfortable and modest recreational areas. The hot afternoon hours, endless naps and a lazy pastime forced the Mediterranean people to seek shelter, and now the whole world is envying their wonderful gardens. Of course, it is impossible to completely recreate a Mediterranean garden in moderate latitudes, however, if you follow the general rules, you can get something completely authentic.

Sometimes small terraces are artificially raised above the ground, creating platforms with round shapes. Sometimes clay or standard paving slabs, wooden floors and ordinary bricks are used as covers. The Mediterranean garden has its own distinctive colors, so pastel, terracotta and ocher are often used in design.

The recreational area of the Mediterranean is decentralized - meaning that not everything is restricted to one balcony or patio. In this garden, you can find some secluded corners with a bench, table, chairs, or small cabin. Any built wall, sprawling tree, gazebos intertwined with ivy or girl vineyards - everything can complement the main entertainment district. All you have to do is put accents - a wicker chair, a fabric chair or a metal seat.

"Stone" motifs must be present throughout the garden. We are talking about different types and types of stone - straw, marble chips, gravel, ceramic and sandstone. It's also a good idea to create many high terraces, walls or stairs made of natural stone, even if they perform an exclusive decorative function.

For "ancient" stones, reminiscent of the times of Roman legion and Greek explorers, you must choose the appropriate antique tools. Garden shapes in the form of cracked or half-broken amphibians and other vessels, decorated with plants that grow directly into them, are a good addition to any composition. The good news is also for those who have not yet acquired good builders.

If any wall or construction collapses - it does not matter. Combinations that have not stood the test of time are only allowed in Mediterranean style.

Palm trees and other exotic plants can be grown in apartments and other enclosed spaces in containers or ponds, and placed outside in the summer. In addition, there is a whole group of plants that are very similar to their Mediterranean counterparts, but they compare favorably with the harshness of winter. The leaves of semi-tropical drought-resistant plants are colored in silver colors (such as olive). The symmetry among the plants that grow in our country is the silver goof. Although it is 4 meters high, its fruits and crown are very similar to the olive tree, which is what people who like to build a garden like the Mediterranean enjoy.

Cottage Garden

The term home garden has become a garden with mostly informal old decorations. Randomly mix and mix plants. Self-sowing flowers, barrel flowers that crawl through rose bushes and plants that fall on the edge of paths are signatures of modern gardening style. It is not uncommon to find edible plants in this mix. Although it may look as if there is no care or design, a successful home garden may require a lot of maintenance, or it will quickly become a complete mess. Today we have many differences in a traditional cottage garden. Most of them are still mostly floral, but with the popularity of edible landscapes increasing in popularity and the size of our yards shrinking, more and more food finds its way into the cottage gardens.

When done well, home gardens blend colors, motifs, shapes, and even perfumes.

If you are not one that follows the rules, then the country style may be the default. There is no concern for spacing, do not worry about planting in odd numbers, and there is no graduation to rise.

But the attraction of the home garden seems clear. Flowers and the scent of the home welcome you and greet you every time you open your door. If you want to surround your home with a homely atmosphere, you can start by simply placing a small bed on either side of the track or driving to your home and continuing to expand it over the years. From there you can add tracks, additional seating areas and other personal touches.

Advantages

Character: there will be no two cottages for the cottage. In fact, there will not be one home garden, two years in a row. The plants will continue to move and the balance between them will recede and flow.

Inexpensive and economical: although you will not get an immediate effect, you can start a cottage garden with a few bundles of seeds and some patience. Even if you outperform some major plants, such as rose bushes or flowering bushes, you can temporarily fill up with cheaper plants.

Self-cultivators will fill quickly, and you can divide and multiply perennials every year. Find a friend or two with the same tastes and swap plants, to expand your palette.

It should not be completely preserved: you will need to keep some order in your garden, or it will quickly become tangled and enlarged. But it does not need to be pure. There is less chance than anyone noticing two weeds or plants that need to be struck.

Country Garden

The innocent nature is the basis of the village park. He does not declare the idea of unity with nature, but rather nature itself.

The free design of the countryside does not mean, however, the complete lack of rules. here they are:

- Simplicity and light randomness,
- Pebbles sprayed or paved with gaps covered with grass,
- Presence of fruit trees and garden beds,
- Flowers grow not only in the flower beds,
- Creeping, climbing plants on fences,
- Decor of "village" things - parts of woven figs, carts, wheels, crockery, jugs, barrels,
- Fruit in the role of flowers - pumpkin, physics, grape brushes and mountain ash,
- Combine horticultural and wild cultures in one group.

The village viewpoint is the middle between the natural neglect , home care, beauty and good.

Fruit trees, shrubs, and beds are required, in this, we can say, style identity. It is best to strictly arrange apples or plums that do not heap, but in different corners of the site. It is also not worth creating a garden full of beds, you can define yourself with healthy herbs and spices.

Expensive precious flowers will not match the scenery, full of rural excitement. But such a garden is irreplaceable from sunflowers, mallow, cosmos, chamomile, and marigolds.

Japanese Garden

Through these basic steps, bring the Japanese feeling to your garden. First, embrace the ideal of nature. This means making things in the garden as natural as possible, and avoid including things that destroy the natural appearance.

For example, do not include square pots in the design, because square pots do not exist in nature. Similarly, if you compare a waterfall with a fountain, the waterfall will be closer to nature. Therefore, you must also consider the Japanese Sumi or Balance concept. Because one of the main purposes of Japanese garden design is to reproduce the large landscape even in the smallest places. Be careful when choosing items for your garden, because you don't want to eventually fill a large stone with 10 x

10 yards.

As a miniature landscape, rocks in the garden represent mountains and ponds represent lakes. A space filled with sand will represent the ocean. By doing this, we assume that the gardener is looking for a minimalist way to better express it with the phrase "less is more".

About garden accessories

Let us consider the park as a microcosm of nature. If we regard the garden as a real haven, we must "isolate" it from the outside world. Therefore, fences and gates are an important part of Japanese gardens.

Fences and gates are both symbolic and functional. The fears and worries in our daily life must still remain in this independent world, the garden. The fence protects us from outside influences, and the gate is the threshold for us to get rid of our daily worries and then prepare to face the real world again. The use of fences is based on the concept of hidden/exposed or Miegakure. The fence pattern is very simple and placed through screen planting, so there is not much clue about what is hidden in it. If this is the case, you can cut a small window on the steel wall around the garden as a sample of the garden. Sode-gaki or sleeve fence is a fence tied to the building structure, and only a specific view of the garden can be seen from inside the house.

Modern Garden

This kind of garden styles is purely based on a geometric layout and relies on scale and proportion to add drama even if in the use of decorative ornaments is not present. This design is generally exemplify by free-owing spaces as most of the design principles in landscaping is not followed such as the lines, horizontal and vertical as well as the symmetry. It focuses more on the materials that will use or the architectural plan itself rather than on plants. As to the material palette, it is kept to a minimum with smooth concrete used for walls or paving and limestone or slate. This style often favored large slabs to build uninterrupted, clean surfaces. Planting tends also to be limited mostly to specimen trees, lawns, clipped hedges, and large blocks of simple plantings with architectural specimens. Reflective pool brings light into the garden and provides serene surfaces.

Urban Garden

Many urban gardens have unique shapes and sizes. The L-Shape is one of the most common. This shape can be challenging to work with because the view from the side return is often bland and the space is too small to place a deck or an outdoor room.

The first step is to define the spaces. Your goal in this elegant garden design is to create a garden that is full of interest in a very small space. Planting is the most obvious solution, but planting does take up quite a bit of room which means you should only plant items that act as architectural showpieces.

This leaves you with hard landscaping and changing the materials you use. You can create a quite space that is hidden from view, protected from wind, and can act as your seating area. No garden is complete without one. In awkwardly shaped gardens, you can add half-walls that will hug your outdoor benches or seating area.

For urban gardens, your design should be simple but make the most out of the space you have. This is where you can play with angles to add a great deal of detail. Try putting in a deck which runs in one direction and then add lines from a paved area that run in the other direction. The eye is naturally drawn to the lines and this plays a visual trick on your guests: it creates the impression that your garden is much longer than it is.

Pick plants that are in leaf all season. Because your space is limited, you want plants that will grow all year round. You can break up the landscape with paving or a small deck, or even a row of colorful shrubs or small trees.

If you have a fence you can paint it or stain it a bright color. White will make your small garden seem bigger and bright colors can show off the garden furniture you have or the plants you have. If you want to create a modern look, consider somber grey colors to contrast your plants.

Narrow Garden

Narrow garden applies when your home has thin and long outdoor spaces. This design is ideal for anyone too busy to garden regularly. It is planted with various low-maintenance shrubs such as Euonymus and Hebe. It also means that there is no grass to cut, and the borders but an occasional trim only. This design breaks up a long garden with short pathways, each one leading to a shapely plant, such as a standard box or a curvaceous pot. The two wide and a smaller pergola will give the impression of width as it will look wider. It also helps provide the garden with shade and screen and privacy secluded seating area at the end of the plot.

Formal Garden Style

Due to the weakness of humans in nature, this garden style is often illustrated by intensive structure and architecture. Organized by a central node or path, formal garden designs typically focus on identities and it is effortlessly recognizable land patterns. This axis is often marked by decorative or sculpture ornament and fulcrum. The material slab is usually kept to a bare minimum with regular paving stones and gravel. The main agricultural features are hedges and lawns, the latter being used for space degradation, boundary borders or the creation of a kindergarten. Add height, Vulgar trees can be introduced to create neat streets, while the decorative borders can be cultivated to alleviate the rigid geometry of the garden.

Family Garden

Having this kind of garden style is very inexpensive especially on the plants that you wanted to grow to your yard. Compared to buying expensive vegetables like broccoli this cost $4, this will save you money. This does not really follow some design elements due to the collective designs idea made by your family. The plants that usually grow in family garden are more likely fruits and vegetables and flowers. What's more good to this is you can plant the crops together with your family, even your kids can do that. So here are the steps on how to start a family garden.

Step 1: You have to pick a great spot for your garden design.

This is very crucial to the success of your garden. You have to find a great spot to set it up considering the areas where there's a need of sunlight for your particular plants and shade for other plants. It was very important it depended a lot on the types of the plants you want to grow because if it was placed wrongly the plants may die and waste not only your money but also your efforts. To do this, pick a sketchbook and then draw out your plans. You have to make notes where each plant should go with that you can also see if the area is big enough.

Step 2: Combined all ideas suggested by everyone

This is considered to be a family project, so it is also important to consider your kid's suggestion. So, families have to brainstorm to come up with great ideas. Always have a list for the suggestions made. Brainstormed ideas of what we wanted to plant and kept a running list.

Step 3: Set a budget for it.

For the money won't go on waste, you have to set a budget and stick to it. There's a lot of ways how to stick on to it. For example, instead of buying a fully grow plants which cost is too much, go for the seeds ones. With that you can plant it together with kids and the cost of it is low. Be practical and wise in looking and buying for materials

Step 4: Have a scheduled chores

To keep your plants be well-maintained, make a schedule for who will be in charge of what and when in the entire gardening process. With this, it will help the members of the family be responsible and involved. You can create a "Garden Chore Chart" this includes things like weeding, watering, fertilizing and so on. It's a simple concept and in return it will keep the kids engaged throughout the year.

Natural & Foliage Garden

The essence of the project lies in the minimal infiltration of the natural environment in order to preserve the maximum natural nature possible.

Natural garden is a local, self-contained ecosystem in which all elements are connected and supported. Its signs are:

- Materials of natural origin typical for the region;

- Originality, miraculous relief.

- A mixture of flower garden with wild plants, plants and stones.

- Natural lawns, grass is not covered with grass, wild, field;

- Careless rough intermittent tracks with gaps lined with stones;

- Forest trees and shrubs.

The basis of the garden is the feature of the plants in the region and not only because it meets the norms of the natural cap. But also because these plants are pest resistant and do not require chemical protection.

Tracks covered with stone, grass or gravel - they should not be straight, but they should not be winding, so they do not protrude from the environment.

Environmental design features are rudimentary furniture made of wood, wicker, rattan, stone fireplace, fireplace, cottage or shed. Tree trunks, obstacles, and saw trees in the eco garden are replaced with benches and statues, and a small swamp bordered by reeds is replaced by a fountain.

Garden decor not visible: lanterns, for example,

from hanging bottles from trees, bird feeders or wicker or hemp crafts. Decorate the ecological site, the house of the beetles, and the cell.

The Garden palette is soft natural colors.

Productive Garden

You don't need a great place to develop a garden. If containers are used, no specific land is required. Whether you are using land or a container, there are four important things to consider: Place the garden not far from home so that you can collect fresh vegetables and ensure that there is plenty of sunlight in the garden (six hours or more). And there are water sources and the most important soil nearby. A small garden plot of 10 feet x 15 feet may be enough to get started. Remember, you must clear the weeds and plant the garden to succeed.

When you sit down and decide what vegetables to grow in the productive garden, please don't be taken away. Get a seed catalog, review it, and choose your favorite vegetables. Limit it to a small amount of vegetables. Making choices will allow you to spend time in the garden and provide the best care. It is easy to grow green onions, zucchini, cucumbers, peas and green beans. It makes sense to choose a variety of vegetables as a backup and determine which group grows best in your environment.

Intensive crops use many nearby farming techniques in specific areas. Plants can grow into strips one to four feet wide. Another method is to divide the space into square parts while leaving space between the parts. Concentrated crops usually reserve space by placing more plants in a square area of the space; however, nearby crops require weeding. Garden design software can also replace garden layout.

Another method is to build a bunk bed. The bunk bed is just a garden mound formed on a flat bed. The elevated bed is made of wood, brick or concrete blocks and soil. Use wood, brick or concrete blocks to create a square or rectangular

frame and fill it with garden soil. Garden soil should be a suitable mixture of soil and organic matter.

If you decide to plant the garden in soil instead of tall containers or beds, the soil should be crushed (and loose). It can be cultivated manually with a trowel (garden trowel) or a mechanical plow. Using a plow will cause you to produce sludge in the soil. Soda should be removed before leveling the soil. In either case, the soil should be loose to a depth of 8 to 12 inches. The soil should be smooth and stateless. Do not pack the soil after farming. Finally, before sowing, the soil should be watered and allowed to stand for a few days.

It is now time to decide whether to plant the seeds or to start with the earlier seeds or buy plants from the nursery. Using prefabricated plants can ensure that your crops are harvested as early as possible. Some vegetables should be seeded, such as beans and peas.

Home gardening is a popular period for nearly one-third of the population. Productive gardening is a type of home gardening that reduces pain and helps to have a significant impact on your food bill. Only a few simple steps, you can easily achieve a home garden. These steps include: selecting a location, deciding which plant to plant, setting the outline, and using seeds and seedling preparation locations.

CHAPTER 3
Build Your Garden

Building Garden Structure: Patios, Walks, Walls Etc.

Patios and decks

Having patios and decks are wonderful additions to your garden landscaping ideas. With this, you can completely be a part of the considerable room that could be extending outwards. So you need to choose the portion of your house where you want the finest landscape for your patio or deck. As you see, there are plenty of homeowners who benefit from having terraces or decks since these are said to be the great places to unwind and mix with family. Your deck and patio should be based on your landscaping ideas for your main garden. You can also include some tiles and roads to walk from the main room to the patio or deck.

Structures as Stones and Water

Stone structures make up most of the garden Calgary landscaping ideas. These are created by fixtures or even prepared of water structures. They are completed to endure even the heaviest essentials a's stone can last even during heavy rain or hot weather. Garden landscaping ideas can also contain water structures. These are frequently created as ponds, pools, waterfalls and fountains.

Walls and Fences

Aside from making your garden safe, walls and fences also compliment your garden design. Walls can also be familiarized mark roads and boundaries.

Light

The right amount of lightning allows you to build different moods. Although often used for the period of the darkness, appropriate lighting, the beauty of your garden and can enhance an artwork in the night. Fixing up your landscaped garden can be difficult. When you come out with a prettily landscaped garden, you'll be glad about the time you expended on it and you can benefit from a number of hours to see the fruits of your work.

Back yard buildings

Outdoor Rooms

A stylish outdoor room is a unique hideaway for any elegant garden. In its most basic form, an outdoor room offers a shelter from unpredictable weather. You can create a semi-enclosed or fully enclosed space in which to serve drinks or hors d'oeuvres. The structure does not need to be complex. In fact, it can be very simple.

You can find any sized structure to fit your needs. A basic, G-box offers a variety of doors and windows and is pre-wired electrically. The cost for the complete room is roughly forty five thousand dollars. You can create a spa type room with saunas that let in the natural sunlight during the day, or you can make it a greenhouse room.

In order to add value to your property with an outdoor room in the elegant garden the room must have power, and remain warm and dry especially for the winter months. But of course, the more elaborate the outdoor room, the more you will need to plan and the higher the cost Be honest and true with yourself before you start making the plans and looking at different rooms.

Is there space in your elegant garden for an outdoor room or will it takes up the majority of your yard?

Remember that an elegant garden is more appealing to potential buyers than an outdoor sauna room that takes up ninety percent of the lawn. You can of course, invest in a temporary structure that can be moved from time to time. Most people install these rooms along the bottom of their garden. However, if the bottom of your garden lines a road, you may need to seek special permission. If you opt to place it in the center of your garden, it might look odd as the focal point unless you complement it with landscaping.

If you place it somewhere that is in the shade, prepare for the room to get cold and install a form of heating and lighting to compensate for no natural light. Some outdoor rooms have an EC SmartGlass glaze that will change from clear glass to black in order to improve the UV protection and reduce glare. It can transform from clear to black in a matter of minutes.

Some low maintenance outdoor rooms have a grass roof which is ecofriendly and keeps the costs for cooling and heating on the inside relatively low. Practically speaking, you may need plumbing and electrics inside of this outdoor garden escape which will need to be connected to the facilities inside of your home. You may also need under floor heating if you plan to spend a lot of time in the outdoor room or a surface heater if you only plan to visit periodically.

In terms of light, keep the furniture light in color and construction. Heavy furniture will seem out of place. Also, the more windows for your outdoor room, the better, especially if it is in the center of your elegant garden escape.

Outdoor Kitchens

An outdoor kitchen is a wonderful way to enjoy the outdoors. Have you ever noticed food tastes better when you eat outside? It's a perfect opportunity to add lines, form, scale, color and texture - all the basic elements! - in your landscape design.

If you're constructing an outdoor kitchen, keep in mind you're going to need power if you're installing a refrigerator, TV, sound system, ice maker, and plumbing if you're installing a sink or a dishwasher.

* Consider the location of your outdoor kitchen. With a grill facing West, it's going to be brutal for the cook in the late afternoon.

* Install your appliances just as you would an indoor kitchen. Functional. Install a dishwasher next to the sink. Allow plenty of counter space to prepare food, next to the grill. You want to be able to move around your outdoor kitchen with ease and functionality.

*If installing a cooktop, make sure you have appropriate ventilation above the cooktop.

* Consider buying a prefab kit. It's easy to DIY install and fairly inexpensive.

The photo above is a prefab outdoor kitchen unit.

For a more detailed outdoor kitchen design, you can find sites that will allow you to create your design, free.

Outdoor Fireplaces or Fire Pits

You can add lines, form, scale, color, and texture to your landscape with a fireplace or fire pit.

* Use your yard, year-round when you install an outdoor fireplace or fire pit.

* Choose a good location. This is going to be a focal point. On your deck or patio? Or maybe create a separate seating area somewhere in your yard.

* Keep size in mind as well as fire precautions - overhead structures.

* You can buy kits, build it yourself, or hire someone to build it for you.

* If you're using propane or natural gas, keep in mind you'll need to run the line under ground from the source to your fire pit or fireplace.

Front yard buildings

Fountains and Waterworks

A sure way to add interest in one's garden and to mimic the scenes in nature is to have a working waterworks system. You can have fountains in any size, with statues spouting water into a pool. You could have mini waterfalls or simulated streams which aside from being visually attractive, give off that gentle soothing sound of rushing water. You

could make use of an underground spring or river by building a well. Aside from being a possible water source, it could be a thing of beauty as well.

Ponds and Bridges

One way of getting close to nature is to create habitats for living creatures. One of the most commonly made is a fishpond. It is a great way to house your aquatic animal friends while creating little spots of attractive landscaping. If the pond or pool is big enough, one may even put in a bridge for better viewing and feeding of the fishes, and to get you from one side to the other. Having ponds is a good way of nourishing aquatic flora and fauna as well. You can have water lilies or lotuses to beautifully spruce up the surface of the pond or pool.

Animal Feeders, Habitats, and Baths

Aside from creating habitats, another way of attracting animal life is by creating feeders and baths. The most common one would probably be bird baths and bird feeders, but there are other types that could be made to attract a wider variety of wildlife. Instead of putting birdfeed, you could put in nuts and grains for squirrels. You could make a beehive feeder to attract potential plant pollinators. With the types of plants and trees that you have in the garden, you can possibly attract or

repel certain kinds of birds, bats, insects, and a variety of small rodents. This is not a bad thing, as they can help in fertilization, pollination, and spread of the plant species.

CHAPTER 4
Plant & Materials Guide

Materials Guide

Small shovel:

A small shovel is perfect for pots. It makes it simple to dig in fertilizers and also to plant your crops or seeds in the pot.

Hand Weeder:

A hand weeder is a small fork class of tool with a long neck. It's useful for planting seeds and small plants and removing the little weeds that grow in containers. It can be used to dig a tiny hole to put the plant or seed.

Plant containers:

A plant container is a container for the crops, and it has to be the right size. You can make use of any container for growing plants and vegetable crops.

Wooded boxes or crates, gallon-sized coffee cans, old washtubs, as well as five-gallon buckets can be used for growing vegetables in as much as there is sufficient drainage.

Small cups or egg Cartons to start seeds:

You can use this for sprouting seeds. Ascertain your container is sufficiently broad to give room for the seeds to germinate. If you do not have enough space, the plants have to be transplanted as they grow. Also, you may need to buy a seed heating device as most times you a required to sprout them within, for it to be adequately warm so that they can germinate and grow.

Soil:

Quality potting soil is a determinant for your plants to grow well. That is the secret to a successful container garden. If you use poor soil, your plants or seeds will not grow. The soil means a lot. Make sure you get top quality soil that your plants require to thrive with or without fertilizer.

Plant seeds:

A plant seed can be flower or vegetable seeds. The ideal thing is to look for high-quality seeds if you are to plant vegetables to be able to harvest seeds and keep for another season. Determinate tomatoes and shrub type plants grow brilliantly well in

containers. If you're looking forward to the best crops in your pots, go for these types of plants.

Garden Gloves:

Though garden glove may not be very essential if you are the type that easily got disgusted by dirt and didn't want stain beneath your nails, or sensitive to some particular plants, you need garden gloves. Also if you do not want to lay your hand on a caterpillar, tomato hornworm, snail and gardens insects when removing them from your favorite crops, garden gloves do the job better. It will also guard your hands against thorns or all other sharp components of the plants.

Watering can:

Watering can do the job better by making the task of watering plants simple and trouble-free because water is running out of it in the form of trickling rain. You can, however, make use of a milk jug to convey water outside. But if you are to use it, ensure you gently pour the water in your hand and spread with your fingers to enable the water to scatter and drop softly into the soil. If not, water coming from jug may land heavily on the soil and splash back on the crop's foliage, raising its danger of having fungus issues and other infections.

Trowel:

A trowel is also an essential tool for container gardening. It is being used to loosen up compressed dirt as well as digging through trash in plant containers. Rather than using your hands, the trowel will get the task done better and faster and leave your hand dirt free.

Pruners:

A pruner is useful for cutting off dead foliage and pruning plants. Though you might think of using scissors, it is not advisable to use it. There are wet saps on plants which may leave remains stick and rust on your scissors. Cutting plants with scissors instead of pruner also increase the risk of the plants being infected. Pruner is more active in cutting

thicker crop stems, also enable clean cut while leaving your plants healthier in the containers.

Plant Organic Pesticide:

If you are a non-fastidious type who could squish insects and not have a bad feeling, a pesticide may not be necessary for you. However, if the reverse is the case, it is ideal you have a plant-safe pesticide as part of your tools. Ensure you adhere to all instructions on its usage because it may not be right on food plants. Possibly, you can remove the pest from the plants and spray on the floor with the pesticide.

Stick or String:

These are essential for supporting container plants that needed to be upheld. An example is tomato plants (string and stick or tomato cage can be used to support tomatoes). They can also be used for young trees that needed to be upheld to grow in a straight line up and plants growing up the fence. Stick can be bought at your local garden store. String or yarn could be an organic color, like brown or dark green for it not to stand out in the garden environment.

Quality Fertilizer:

Fertilizer is also essential for the growth of your plant. Having secured good soil, ensure you obtain a high-quality organic fertilizer to get the best

result from crops. Compost can be in pellet or liquid form. You can buy specific fertilizer for each type of your plants like rose or citrus fertilizer. However, an all-purpose plant fertilizer does the job for most gardeners. Compost can as well be used to supplement your crop's feeding

Potting Bench:

A potting bench is also an essential tool for gardeners. Firstly it serves as a platform to assemble and store your small appliances, plant marker, fertilizer, and the likes. You can also use it to conveniently move your planting tools from one place to another (for example, from your kitchen to your garden)

Each of the gardening tools is very important for your container garden to be successful. Make sure have them at your disposal to ease work as well as getting the best results out of your products.

Plant guide

Believe it or not, Latin really is one of your best friends when it comes to learning about plants.Latin is so descriptive, you can gain so much information just by understanding the name. For example, if I see a plant with the word 'repens' in it, I know that means that the plant will grow flat along the ground, because the word 'repens' means creeping or flat in Latin.

You may think that is obvious by looking at a plant, but the plants in garden centers may only just be filling their pot, so it may not be obvious as to its eventual growing habit.

Examples of Helpful Latin Names

- alba means the flowers will be white
- alpina means from the Alps, so will be very hardy
- argentea means it will be silvery
- aurea(s) means that the foliage or flowers will be yellow
- australis means from the south or from Australia, so not frost hardy
- chinensis means the plant is from China so should be fairly hardy
- coccinea means it will have red flowers or berries
- coloumnunaris grows in a, you guessed it, column shape
- decumbens means a small growth habit
- fastigata means the plant has a very upright growth habit
- gigantea means it will be big for that species not necessarily huge
- glauca means it will have blueish coloured foliage

- grandiflora means it will have large flowers
- horizontalis has a similar meaning to repens but taller
- japonica means the plant is from Japan so should be fairly hardy
- latifolia means wide leaves
- longifolia means long leaves
- macrocarpa means large fruits
- macrophylla means large flowers
- marinus means the plant is tolerant of coastal conditions
- nigra means some part of the plant will be black (often the stem)
- officinalis means the plant has medicinal qualities
- pendula foilage hangs down in a 'weeping' fashion
- purpurea means the foliage or flower will be purple
- repens means plant is low growing and spreads across the ground
- rosea means the flowers or sometimes foliage will be pink
- rubra means the flowers or foliage will be reddish

- variegatus means the leaves will be variegated (two-tone foliage)
- villosa means hairy

Latin Names May Help You Choose Plants

By understanding Latin names, when you look through plant availability lists and you come across plants with which you aren't familiar, oftentimes the name alone will give you enough information to know if it's a plant you might want to use.

Not Native? Check Invasive!

One really important thing you need to look at before you introduce any plant into your garden is if it is invasive. In the USA, many popular garden plants are invasive and are escaping from the confines of gardens and damaging natural environments. When native plants are crowded out of their habitats, the wildlife that relies on them for feeding can really suffer which affects the whole ecosystem.

You usually get overly invasive plants that can become pests and take over your garden becoming worse than native weeds. Houttuynia and Physalis immediately spring to mind!

If you're about to buy a plant and you can see it bursting out from its pot in the garden centre, do double check its growth rate before you buy it. There's a good likelihood it might be too vigorous for your garden!

In order to create a beautiful planting design, it is really important to take into account the shape of each plant, its color, size and flowering time as well as what growing conditions it needs. The plant does not only have to be able to thrive in the conditions and environment in which you put it, but it must also look good with the surrounding plants and be the right size.

Creating a successful planting design is worse than trying to do a seating plan for a wedding! Plants cannot get up and move if they don't like who they are next to, so it is critical to get them in the right place at the start.

As successful plant combining is such big topic, I'm going to be writing a separate book on how to effectively combine plants. But until then, just remember if you just choose a plant because you like its flowers but the foliage is ugly, unless it's hidden by other plants, you're going to be looking at the ugly foliage for longer than the nice flowers because plants don't flower all the time!

Buying Plants

Whenever I design a planting scheme, I find out from the local garden centers and nurseries what plants they have available before I start on the planting plan.

When I first started out as a designer, I used to get very carried away and excited with lots of different plants I'd seen in books. Over the years, I've found there is nothing more annoying than spending a lot of time planning the perfect planting scheme only to find that most of the plants are really difficult to get hold of or not available.

Designing a successful planting scheme often involves repeating key plants throughout the scheme. So, it's very helpful if you can buy the quantity of plants you need. Don't worry if you don't know hundreds of plants - the best schemes don't have a million different plant varieties. Keep it simple and repeat the star-performers.

Planting Techniques

Seed starting helps gardeners save a significant amount of money. You can also get to choose from a wider variety of plants and have the freedom to experiment with your garden.

There are many different options available for seed starting. It can be something simple and affordable, or you can go to a more complex and expensive way. It depends entirely on the gardener. You will definitely benefit from the tips given here for seed starting as a beginner. The methods given here will be cost-efficient as well as effective for any beginner at gardening.

Planting Seeds at the Right Time

Before you get into the how of planting seeds, you have to consider the when. You need to time the seed starting in a way that will allow your plants to grow big and strong. This will allow them to withstand the pressure of being uprooted and transplanted into the garden. However, the plants should not grow big enough for them to become root-bound in the seed starting space. Planning ahead and using a calendar will help you figure it out.

First, you have to figure out when the last frost date for your region is. Using this data, you can find the right time to plant your crops in the garden. If you mark down the last frost date and the seed starting

date for each season, you will soon see a pattern emerge. Most areas have two batches for seed starting. The first batch is for crops that grow well in cold weather, and the second batch is for crops that grow well in warm weather. You don't need to be exact for the seed starting dates. You can easily shift the sowing or planting dates around a little when you need it.

Seed Starting Containers

You can buy pots that are used for starting seeds. If you want to save on the expense, you can just recycle any old containers you have. You can easily use any egg cartons, yogurt cups, or plastic party cups for seed starting containers. Clean the containers and just poke holes into the bottom to allow drainage.

You can also use peat pots if you aren't starting too many seeds at once. These peat pots can be planted directly into the ground when you are done. These are a little bit pricey if you plan to start many plants. You have many other options for seed starting, but recycled containers, trays or peat pots will usually do the job for anyone. These are also the most easily available as compared to others.

Medium for Seed Starting

As a beginner, you may think that picking up dirt or mud from anywhere will work for your plants. However, plants actually need specific types of soil

for growth at different stages. For seed starting, you need to get seed starting medium or seed starting soil. It is specifically meant to help seeds grow out of their shell.

Experienced gardeners can prepare their own seed starting soil, but for a beginner, it is better to buy the ready-made variety. Getting a bag or box of seed starting medium from a local supply store will work for you in the beginning. This material also comes in the form of pellets that have to be watered so they can expand and be used for starting seeds. These jiffy discs or pellets are great for getting kids interested in gardening.

Seeds

Now you have to consider the seeds you want to plant.

Planting Techniques

Setting Up the Right Environment for Starting Seeds

The goal here is to set up an environment that is ideal for growing the plants you want in your garden. You have to mimic the natural environment in which they grow well. Most plants grow well when they get enough warmth and sunlight.

How To Plant Seeds

After setting up the right environment and getting the required tools, you can start the actual work of planting the seeds. This does not take much time.

Step 1- Fill the seed container or tray with seed starting medium. Check the instructions on the packaging or the seed-starting medium you use. Accordingly, you will have to wet the soil before or after it goes into the seed container.

Step 2- Plant the seeds. Depending on the seeds you use, you will have to find the right depth to plant them at. Different seeds have to be buried at different depths. Generally, you just have to bury the seed at a depth that is twice its width. There are some seeds that need more light to germinate, so you don't have to bury them into the soil. You just have to plant the seeds on top of the soil to germinate. Pressing them in a little is enough. Most seed packets provide you with this kind of information.

While planting seeds, it is better to plant at least two to three in each spot. There are some seeds that will be duds and not germinate at all. If you plant a few extra seeds, it increases your chances of success in germinating and growing the plant. However, it might also make all the plants grow in the same spot, but this can be thinned out.

Step 3- Give the seeds a good pat-down. Once you plant the seeds, you should give them a little pat in, so they are well seeded inside the soil. It helps to secure the seed in and also allows the seed to recognize its germinating environment.

Step 4- Label the seedlings. If you are growing many plants, you have to label them. It is not possible for you to remember which plant you have planted in each container. Labels will help you keep track and tend to different plants in the appropriate way. You can write directly on the container or use plant markers that can be transferred to the garden along with the plant.

Step 5- Water. If you have wet the seed-starting medium already, you don't need to water it the right way. Check if the soil feels dry and water accordingly. Seeds can get dislodged very easily when you just plant them, so you have to be careful while watering. Using a spray bottle to gently spray water is a better idea than using a watering can. You can also set your hose on mist setting if possible. Use watering cans or heavy watering only after the plant is well established and strong enough to withstand the force.

Step 6- Sprinkle cinnamon on the soil. Cinnamon is very helpful in starting seeds. It helps to prevent the seed from dying due to a bacterial or fungal infection. It is a great tip that organic gardeners

utilize while caring for their plants.

Step 7- Move the seed tray to the right spot. After you have prepared the seeds in their containers or trays, you can move them into their home. Provide them with water and light and wait for the seeds to germinate. Some seeds only take a few days to germinate, but other seeds might even take weeks. You have to be patient and keep checking on seeds every day.

Caring for New Seedlings

Once the seeds have been planted and germinate, you need to care for them every day. Make sure that they are warm and get enough light. You need to check if they require any water or if your pet or child disturbs the plant. There are many beginners who water their plants too much; however, overwatering can also be a problem just like under-watering. Keep checking the top of the soil to see if it looks damp or dry.

If it is damp, you don't need to water the plant. When the top looks dry, you should water it. Stop pouring water when you see it running out of the drainage holes. It gets crusty if the soil is left dry for too long. When you care for your seedlings, keep a spray bottle handy and make sure there is enough moisture in the soil at all times. You can carry out robust watering after germination takes place, and the plant is sturdier.

Germination with Seedlings

When the seeds start to germinate, you will first see the sprout appear at the surface of the soil. You will then see seed leaves or cotyledons emerge. These are not real leaves of the plant but work to gather more nutrients in this phase. A few days after germination, you will see the true leaves of the plant appear. These will be the actual leaves and are larger than the small cotyledons that first appear. The point at which the true leaves appear will signify that the plant is growing well.

Fertilization of Seedlings

You may wonder if seeds or seedlings have to be fertilized at this point. The answer is usually no because the seed starting mix is prepared with all the required nutrients. This mix is enough to help the plant get started. Once the plant has grown properly out of the seed and you pot-up, you can start using fertilizer.

After Thinning Out the Seedlings

Once you have planted and germinated and thinned out the seedlings, you just have to wait and watch the plant grow. Remember to keep the plant well-watered. The more the seedling grows, the more soil the roots will take up, and this will cause it to dry up faster. This means that you might have to water the seedling more frequently. If you use

grow lights to provide light to the plants, make sure that the light is always hanging a couple of inches above the plant. If the plant is getting enough light from the window, you should just rotate the plants a little every day. This will ensure that it is getting light evenly on every part. Without frequent rotation, any plant will start reaching towards the sunlight and may become leggy. If you just keep these things mind, you can sit back and watch as the plant grows.

Potting the Plants

After the seedlings get too big for their seed starter tray or container, you will have to move them. Moving the seedlings to a bigger container or pot is called potting up. Most seedlings don't need potting up unless the plant grows too quickly. Moving it to a bigger pot will allow the plant to have adequate room for growth.

Deciding Which Plants to Pot Up

You may wonder how you can figure out if a seedling needs to be potted up. There are a few signs that will help you determine this. If the plant seems to dry out too fast, it might be because the plant is growing. If you feel like the frequency with which the plant needs watering has increased a lot, you should move it to a larger pot. Another sign is if the leaves on the plant show signs of discoloration.

If a plant uses up all the nutrient mediums, discoloration appears on the leaves due to deficiency. Signs of nutrient deficiency include spotted mottled, yellow, or purple leaves. If you notice this, move the plant to a bigger pot with fresh soil and nutrients. You can also tell that the plant needs to be potted up if it is root-bound. See if the roots of the plant are reaching out through the bottom holes of the container. This means that you need to move the plant to a container with more room for the roots.

Planting Plants and Combination

Full Sun Combination:

Hens & Chicks from the Sempervivum group of succulent plants can easily be grown in a container and make a nice addition to an outdoor space. Hens and Chicks are hardy to zone 4, prefer full sun and are drought tolerant once established. Also, tolerable in extreme temperatures down to -5 degrees, these succulents can be grown in the landscape, such as an addition to a rock garden. When growing these plants as a container garden in colder climates, it is recommended overwintering them either indoors or in a garage, especially if they are in a terra cotta planter, which can be prone to cracking.

Succulent Planter: Photograph taken in Springtime (Full Sun-Drought Tolerant) Sedum Sieboldii Mediovariegatum (top of planter) displays variegated foliage with large light pink blooms appearing in late summer and into fall. In the side pockets are Sedum Angelina (right) which displays

yellow blooms in early summer and Sedum Bertram Anderson (left) which shows off its deep reddish-pink blooms in late summer.

Succulent Planter (Photograph taken in Fall) with Sedum Sieboldii Mediovariegatum, Sedum Angelina and Sedum Bertram Anderson. Foliage and blooms vary throughout the seasons to create constant interest. Succulents require full sun and colors intensify as the summer progresses. Varieties shown are hardy in USDA zones 4-9.

Coleus and Sweet Potato Vine Planter (Sun-Shade)

(1)Obtain a large planter. Either a 16 or 20-inch diameter pot works nicely. Fill with a good potting soil.

(2)Choose a taller variety of Coleus for the center plant.

(3)Plant medium to small sized Coleus of multiple colors in a circular pattern around the larger center plant. Figure six plants for the 20-inch planter.

(4)Pocket Sweet Potato Vine around the perimeter of the pot. For a 20-inch planter, I alternate three of the purple variety and three of the green.

(5)Water, let grow and enjoy! The planter will look fabulous all summer long!

Colorful Coleus Planter

Here is another Coleus combination using a different variety of colors for more of an autumn look. Combine hybrid coleus such as Coleus Rustic Orange and Freckles (variegated yellow and orange) with Dark Star for deep burgundy foliage. Coleus are only hardy in USDA hardiness zone 11 and are generally grown as annuals for their beautiful foliage. They prefer to be grown in partial shade in a moist, but well-drained soil. Some of the newer hybrids of Coleus have been bred to discourage flowering and take more sun, such as the ones used above.

Annual Verbena Planter

Annuals can be used in the garden or in planters to add extra color to your outdoor space during the summer months. Add yellow and red annuals, for example, marigold and geranium to companion with purple verbena.

Annual Tree Lantana

Lantana produces an abundance of brightly colored flowers from summer until fall. It is a tropical evergreen hardy in USDA zones 9-11, requires full sun and a well-drained soil, and thrives on little moisture. Lantana is an attraction for butterflies and hummingbirds, and in cooler climates, is easily grown as either a container plant or annual in your garden.

Face Garden Planter

Add some whimsy to your garden with a decorative planter. Golden Variegated Sweet Flag (evergreen in zones 5-11) creates a look of spiky hair in this garden décor!

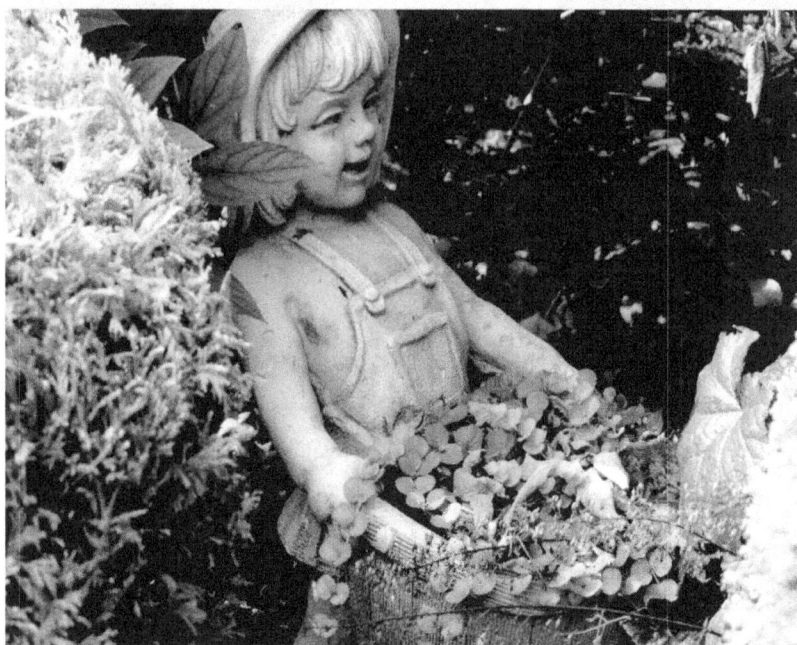

Garden Statuary Planter

Placing statuary in a garden bed can also add a little whimsy to your space. Perennial Creeping Jenny (zones 3-8) trails over this garden gal's planter in a shady area. Behind the planter are 'Palace Purple' Coral Bells (zones 4-9) and to the left is evergreen shrub Gold Mop Cypress (zones 5-7).

Annual Planter Combination (Shade)

In this shade planter combination is (1) Caladium 'White Queen' (2) Red Heartleaf Begonia and (3) Green Sweet Potato Vine, for red blooms and interesting foliage all summer long.

Planter Combination (Sun)

In this planter combination for a sunny location is taller red and yellow Canna Lily (in the backdrop) with sun tolerant, 'Wasabi' Coleus (middle) and trailing New Wave Petunia (front). The Coleus supplies bright lime-green foliage, while Petunia blooms throughout summer. The tall foliage of the Canna Lily towers above the rest of the planter and blooms appear near summer's end. (Note) Sweet Potato Vine and Canna bulbs can be stored for winter and reused the following season.

Plants per Square Meters

Mid-sized Evergreens

This group of plants is very important in residential landscaping as well as the smaller evergreens previously covered. Some homes require larger plants at their foundations due to their height and scale. This group includes plants that can be used for small and medium screens. There could be some overlap in the estimated sizes between this group and the previous group, however, in general this group of plants will be larger.

Common Name	Indica azaleas
Scientific Name	Azalea indica 'Formosa', 'George Tabor', and 'G.G.Gerbing'
Ultimate Height	6'-8'
Ultimate Width	6'-8'
Light Preference	Sun to partial shade
Soil Preference	Tolerant to various soils
Shape	Spreading and mounding
Notes	I think this group of azaleas is a great group of plants because they have vigorous root systems and they have a late blooming period (so frost will not shorten the blooming period). The foliage of these azaleas look better than other azaleas during the rest of the year.

Common Name	**Emerald Green Arborvitae**
Scientific Name	Thuja occidentalis 'Emerald'
Ultimate Height	10'-15'
Ultimate Width	2'-3'
Light Preference	sun
Soil Preference	Well drained
Shape	Upright and pyramidal
Notes	This upright conifer will remain green during the winter unlike some of the other upright conifers. This plant is fairly tame in it growth habit and well suited for the scale of residential landscaping.

Common Name	**American boxwood**
Scientific Name	Buxus sempervirens
Ultimate Height	10'-10'
Ultimate Width	10'-10'
Light Preference	Partial shade to shade
Soil Preference	Well drained with organic matter present
Shape	Rounded habit
Notes	If there is a "king" of the plants, it would be the American boxwood. This slow growing plant has a dark green color and a soft, fine leaf texture. If you have the correct conditions, there is no substitute for this plant

Common Name	**Camellia sasanqua**
Scientific Name	Camellia sasanqua
Ultimate Height	6'-10' depending on cultivar
Ultimate Width	6'-10' depending on cultivar
Light Preference	Sun to partial shade
Soil Preference	Tolerant to various soils
Shape	Upright and spreading (unless pruned)
Notes	Hands down.... This is my favorite group of plants. It is a sturdy evergreen and blooms in the fall (for 4-6 weeks) when every other plant is shutting down for the year.

Common Name	**Lantana**
Scientific Name	Lantana camara
Ultimate Height	2-4' depending on the cultivar
Ultimate Width	2-4'
Light Preference	Full sun
Soil Preference	Well drained soil
Shape	mounding
Notes	This prolific flowering plant loves the heat and performs better as it gets hotter in the summer. When most plants are suffering, lantana is hitting its stride.

Common Name	**Verbena**
Scientific Name	Verbena canadensis
Ultimate Height	1'
Ultimate Width	6'
Light Preference	Full sun
Soil Preference	Well drained
Shape	spreading
Notes	This heavy bloomer comes in several colors and will bloom more if the old flowers are removed.

Common Name	**Sage, Salvia**
Scientific Name	Salvia sp.
Ultimate Height	2-4' depending on the species
Ultimate Width	2-3'
Light Preference	Full sun
Soil Preference	Well drained
Shape	upright
Notes	This is a broad family of plants that love the heat and can extend the blooming in your garden into the fall.

Common Name	**Russian Sage**
Scientific Name	Peroskia atriplicifolia
Ultimate Height	3'
Ultimate Width	3'
Light Preference	Full sun
Soil Preference	Well drained soil
Shape	Loose and irregular
Notes	Blue blooms combine with aromatic grey foliage to be garden standout.

Common Name	**Rosemary**
Scientific Name	Rosmarinus officinalis
Ultimate Height	4'
Ultimate Width	4'
Light Preference	Full sun
Soil Preference	Well drained soil
Shape	Erect branching
Notes	This is another aromatic plant that produces light blue flowers. It is edible as well.

Common Name	**Wand flower**
Scientific Name	Gaura lindheimeri
Ultimate Height	2-3'
Ultimate Width	2-3'
Light Preference	Full sun
Soil Preference	Well drained soils
Shape	Whispy branching
Notes	This is a prolific flowerer and comes back each year stronger than the year before.

Common Name	**Wormwood**
Scientific Name	Artemesia ' Powis Castle'
Ultimate Height	2-3'
Ultimate Width	2-3'
Light Preference	Full sun
Soil Preference	Well drained soils
Shape	Irregular and spreading
Notes	The silver foliage is a nice addition to tie all the blooming plants in your garden together.

Common Name	**Cone flower**
Scientific Name	Echinacea purpurea
Ultimate Height	2-3'
Ultimate Width	2'
Light Preference	Full sun
Soil Preference	Well drained soils
Shape	Upright stalks
Notes	This plant gives nice cut flowers during the summer. Deadhead the spent flowers to promote more flowering.

Common Name	**Foxglove**
Scientific Name	Digitalis x mertonensis
Ultimate Height	2-3'
Ultimate Width	2'
Light Preference	Full to partial sun
Soil Preference	Well drained soils
Shape	Spikes that rise out of a rosette of foliage
Notes	This is the south's version of the delphinium.

Common Name	**Lamb's ear**
Scientific Name	Stachys byzantina
Ultimate Height	1-2'
Ultimate Width	2'
Light Preference	Full sun
Soil Preference	Well drained soils
Shape	Leafy and spreading
Notes	The silver, hairy folige is a nice accent plant for the front of the border.

Common Name	**Lamb's ear**
Scientific Name	Stachys byzantina
Ultimate Height	1-2'
Ultimate Width	2'
Light Preference	Full sun
Soil Preference	Well drained soils
Shape	Leafy and spreading
Notes	The silver, hairy folige is a nice accent plant for the front of the border.

Common Name	**Aster**
Scientific Name	Aster dumosus
Ultimate Height	1-2'
Ultimate Width	1-2'
Light Preference	Full sun
Soil Preference	Well drained soils
Shape	mounding
Notes	This is a nice fall blooming companion plant for salvias, mums, and sedums.

Common Name	**Shasta daisy**
Scientific Name	Leucanthum x superbum
Ultimate Height	3'
Ultimate Width	3'
Light Preference	Full sun
Soil Preference	Well drained soils
Shape	upright
Notes	This is a summer blooming staple of any perennial garden. White daisy flowers are borne on long stalks.

Common Name	**Threadleaf coreopsis**
Scientific Name	Coreopsis verticillata
Ultimate Height	1-2'
Ultimate Width	2-3'
Light Preference	Full sun
Soil Preference	Well drained soils
Shape	mounding
Notes	Covered with 1" flowers throughout the summer. Deadheading will prolong flowering.

Common Name	**Lenten Rose**
Scientific Name	Helleborus x hybridus
Ultimate Height	1-1.5'
Ultimate Width	1.5'
Light Preference	Shade
Soil Preference	Well drained with organic matter present
Shape	Arching foliage
Notes	If you like subtle colors, you will like the color palette that exists in this family.

Common Name	**Bee Balm**
Scientific Name	Monarda x 'Jacob Cline'
Ultimate Height	4'
Ultimate Width	4'
Light Preference	Full sun
Soil Preference	Well drained
Shape	Upright stalks
Notes	This plant spreads and can get powdery mildew, but the flowers are stunning.

Common Name	**Garden phlox**
Scientific Name	Phlox paniculata
Ultimate Height	2-3'
Ultimate Width	2'
Light Preference	Full sun
Soil Preference	Well drained soils
Shape	Stalks terminating in flowers
Notes	This is a nice plant for the back of the flower bed. If it like the spot, this plant could be an aggressive spreader.

Common Name	**Maiden grass**
Scientific Name	Miscanthus sp.
Ultimate Height	4-6'
Ultimate Width	2-3'
Light Preference	Full sun
Soil Preference	Well drained soils
Shape	Grassy clumps
Notes	This group of grasses is suited for the average urban landscape. They do not become too large over time like pampas grass.; Most flower in the fall which extends the garden interest.
Common Name	**Fountain grass**
Scientific Name	Pennisetum alopecuroides
Ultimate Height	3-4'
Ultimate Width	2-3'
Light Preference	Full sun
Soil Preference	Well drained soils
Shape	Grassy clumps
Notes	Smaller than the maiden grass family, fountain grass species are good plants for smaller gardens.

CHAPTER 5
Need Help?

What Difference Can A Designer Make?

The designer greatly arranges everything in an aesthetically pleasing way and they create interesting shapes that make the garden (backyard) look bigger, more interesting and stunning to look at. The patio won't just be an assortment of slabs; it will be shaped in a way that enhances the rest of your garden. The same goes for the shape of the lawn and plant borders.

Take a look at the photographs below. On the left you will see a perfectly decent new patio. It's not been designed, just laid down to a size the owners thought they wanted. Now, here is the comparison made by the designer and not. Look at the difference a designer can make to a boring patio and lawn in the photograph on the right. The brick and curves detail make it much more interesting and pleasing to look at.

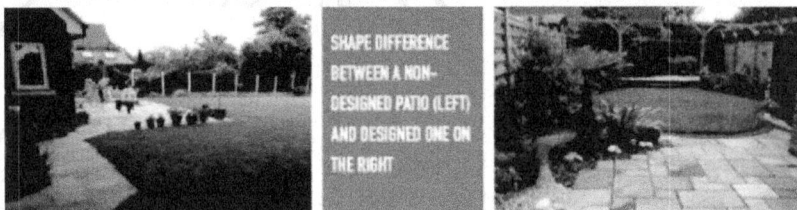

SHAPE DIFFERENCE BETWEEN A NON-DESIGNED PATIO (LEFT) AND DESIGNED ONE ON THE RIGHT

How to Choose the Best Designer for Me?

There are many different types of designer. Some have a fixed style of designing; others can do multiple styles of design, from traditional formal, to modern, contemporary gardens.

The main question is does their work excite, impress or wow you? If it doesn't, move along to the next one. Sounds obvious, but so many people call the first person they come across in Yellow Pages, and they don't always get the results they were hoping for.

If the 'before' photos of the designer's work looks better than the 'after' photos, run away as fast as you can!

Find out the rough of cost a design and whether it is within your budget. Some designers won't give you a price until they've seen the garden (it is difficult to price accurately until seen). Ask for a ballpark, or average design amount, for whatever size garden you have.

If you don't know how big your garden is, pace it

out before you phone so you can give the designer a good idea of the size. No two people have the same perception of small, medium and large; believe me on that one. I've seen quite large gardens described as small and vice versa!

How Much Cost A Good Designer?

Now that's a difficult question to answer definitively, it all depends on the designer and level of their experiences, the location as well as a zillion other factors. Most people say that the design fee is equivalent to the 1/10 or 10% of the cost of the entire garden needed to build. So a £35,000 garden will cost £3,500 ($4,000 US approx) in design fees. I don't find that a totally accurate guide but I think it's okay start.

Now, I will throw out a figure of a minimum of £500 ($750) as a starting point for a good design. In reality, some designers will charge less than that, most will be more. Let's look at the behind the scenes reasons.

How to Get a Cheaper Design

If your finances simply won't stretch to the cost of a design and you know that you don't have the time or inclination to learn it for yourself, well, there are a couple of things you can take into consideration.

First option is the Students! Colleges are always looking for an actual practice where students can execute what they've learned from their course. So, if you are willing to have students walking around your property with a tape measure and clipboard on their hand, this could be a good option for you.

How good the finished design is will usually depend on how advanced the students are and how much help they've had from their subjects they have acquired and the design is unlikely to be quite the same standard as experienced designer though.

Design students may make mistakes. So you will need some design knowledge to know that what they have given you will work.

The second option isn't that far away from the first - hire someone that is recently qualified and needs to build up their portfolio. Again, you need to watch for mistakes and over-imaginative creations that may be difficult to build. But as long as you have some knowledge, it's a great way to help a designer become established and get yourself a much cheaper design. And a newbie will really want to impress you and they will take great care of what they produce for you.

Before you go down that route, I would still speak to an established designer first, and see what they offer - some design students do come straight out

of college and think they will be able to charge the same rates as more experienced designers. So make sure you are getting a real bargain, not an inexperienced designer charging what they'd like to earn!

Postal design services

A third option for getting a discounted design is using a postal garden design service. These are cheaper because the designer doesn't come and visit you on site. It does mean that you have to provide them with an accurate plan to work from and photographs.

A good designer can come up with a great scheme from just a plan and a good set of photos and your design brief. Again, though, do check you like their work before you hire them. As services like this tend to be paid for upfront or in two phases, see if they use a payment merchant like Paypal that will settle disputes if you're not happy with the end results.

CONCLUSION

Thank you for reading this book!

I wrote this book to give you informative ideas on how you will design your yard. Growing plants can be exciting for the home gardener – not only can you implant new plants from your current landscape favorites, but with the aid of this guidebook you can get a head start on your garden, or expand it indoorsv entirely.

Garden Designing is at the base of successful landscaping. Make your vision a true with the support of our garden design ideas, principles, and inspiration for the front yards and backyards. And enhancing your house's landscaping is a great way to increase your properties' attractiveness, and you can create areas outdoors for leisure and entertainment. If you choose to concentrate on improving your curb appeal on a reimagined front yard, build a backyard resort on eating and gathering areas, or both, there are several options and amenities to consider.

You can create an entertainment area in the backyard for friends and relatives, complete with an outdoor patio, fire element, swimming pool, and more, or you can start building lush greenery that helps to draw wild animals and enables you to relax and think. In the front yard, with a lovely walkway, you can either turn up the resale value or pull your grass out for an eco-sustainable landscape. Make the community proud by creating a beautiful and welcoming front yard landscape.

These ideas regarding landscape architecture are important to the design of a scheme that you will appreciate in the years ahead. You can get these ideas about garden designing and landscaping from the following procedures:

See what a lot of people do with their home design designs. If appropriate, speak to them about the reasons behind their choice for home landscaping products, and their feelings.

Newspapers, magazines, television, and the internet do provide a wealth of information regarding what "online" types of home landscape designs really are.

Ask specialist consult for the area of landscape architecture

If you don't want to pay for guidance to a landscape planner, try some tips from your nearest nursery, at least.

You can put into considerations the five key elements that will create a comfortable and enjoyable outdoor living area when properly implemented in your design.

- Line-Lines and geometric patterns can facilitate directional movement across the landscape and highlight important aspects of your space.

- Scale-An array of complementary pattern colors can bring together the entire yard.

- Scale-It is important to select suitably scaled plants and trees to the rest of the surrounding landscape.

- Texture-The different textures of leaves , stems and petals add more detail to the design of your garden.

- Form-The plant life's shape and physical attributes within the design generate natural patterns that give your outdoor space appeal and style.

The landscape design principles are the fundamental concepts used to incorporate the aforementioned garden design elements.

- Unity-One of the most important aspects of custom landscape design with a professional appearance is to create unity throughout your outdoor living area as well as the interior of your home.

- Repetition-Repetition and rhythm are generated by the use of color and texture, creating simple patterns in nature that bring a sense of relaxation and tranquility to your outdoor design.

- Focalization-Lines, shapes and shapes are used to construct focalization points and direct attention to central landscape focal points.

- Balance – Working with these other design principles to balance and symmetry creates a uniform appearance that invites pleasure and pleases the senses.

- Transition-Equally important is the transition and flow of design and each of its components.

- Proportion – Proportion, which is closely related to size, is also one of the basic landscape design criteria.

Next is to find out what area you live in that growing area. The zone indicates which plants in your area are "hardy." For example, I wouldn't plant delicate orchids in my yard as they would freeze and die over the months of cold weather. Dead plants are not making a nicer yard! The type of grass you want to grow is a big consideration. Want to have a Kentucky Bluegrass or Bentgrass carpet?

If your yard is shady and you live in the north, you might want a beautiful Fescue. A nicer yard has luscious grass to go barefoot in!

Investing in landscaping is a good idea for making a yard more appealing. Doing this will greatly enrich the whole appeal of a home. Because of their outward appearance, everyone in the neighborhood will enjoy looking at the house. If somebody wants to make a home's exterior more beautiful, there are a few steps a person can take to do just that.

Especially when someone moves into a house, some external work will always be done to it. If this is the situation, don't be too quick to take it all up. In fact, more often than not, there is something that a person can do with the already existing plants. They should get access to what they already have before a person buys something. That will save both money and time for the individual.

Water gardening is a very beautiful style of gardening, which has been around for years and followed. The water garden can be designed either in an existing water source or in an artificially induced water system. The water garden that has been created becomes complete even when it's visible from our living area and gives us fun. A water garden offers many possibilities to plant and grow. You can start small, with a boiled-out stone trying

to collect in-ground storage tank, a watertight, patio-sized vessel, or dive in with a lily, fish, and shower right in. You need to do some researches before you create a water garden to assess your severity and style.

Rome was not built in a day. The same goes for the landscaping of your garden. Its basic concepts are important when it comes to landscaping. Once you have all the preliminary checks, all you have to do is to wait. Wait for the seeds to bloom on beautiful bushes and see how your garden blooms in different shades of color over time.

We hope this will help you learn about the landscape and given you some ideas. We hope you enjoyed experimenting with your lawn and garden. Let your neighbors envy your picturesque garden! Thanks again for purchasing!